CW00664228

UPWELLING

HAIKU, SENRYU, TANKA AND HAIBUN

Lorraine A Padden

UPWELLING

Text © 2022 Lorraine A Padden
www.lorrainepadden.com
Art © 1982, 2022 Penelope Padden

ISBN 978-1-958408-06-3

Red Moon Press
PO Box 2461
Winchester VA
22604-1661 USA
www.redmoonpress.com

Cover: Penelope Padden
"Tied to the Dock" (1982)
Woodblock print 2/6, 10" x 11"
Used with permission.

first printing

In gratitude for the legacy
of traditional Japanese short form poetry,
and to its contemporary fluidity
that invites marginalized moments to inhabit
a rightful place on the page.

lane markers
another haiku
crosses the line

UPWELLING

My husband asks if I happen to know why the distance between the World Trade Center Twin Towers was slightly greater at the top than at the bottom of the two buildings.

from the couch to the floor

He says, "You can't see it, but the towers were actually designed that way."

they close their eyes

I flash back to a memory of standing in Tobin Plaza, craning my neck to follow the lines of the towers as far as I could. Then it hits me. "The curvature of the earth."

and jump

another Sunday
without a Bible
unbroken snow

out
of
body
experience

the long drive

out
of
Texas

clipped wings the hallway chatter about makeup

back to school special!

on flak jackets and masks

schoolyard bully

a chocolate milk mustache

The Bronco's on and off the brakes so I ease up to leave more room between us. Some swerving each time the driver reaches over to tend to what I imagine must be an excited puppy in the passenger seat.

play date

He pulls over to the curb so everyone behind him can make their way around.

the sound of marbles

Those curious dog ears suddenly become the tousled hair of a young boy cowering as Bronco lifts himself out of his seat and leans over with both hands.

hitting the floor

petals turn
pink to violet
the other cheek

down girl
he says to his dog
performance review

black-eyed susan
the garden
she left behind

bindweed
pinky swearing
to silence

lingering heat

he decides

not to throw

a second punch

white daffodils
around a pedophile's grave
daughter bulbs

d
r
i
p
p
i
n
g
faucet

over and

over and

over

his opinion

the thrust of his rebuttal
in the body
of her email

backed up sewer line

the #MeToo movement

tuition you said lap dance

hide and seek
before the countdown
he tells me
the pink tights
might give me away

saddling
her
the
tight
breast
collar

RBG
the outspoken pattern
of a lace collar

cloister walls
the impetus
of a climbing rose

The action shot taken in the studio opens an article about a female choreographer working on her next debut. Halfway through the piece it's revealed she's had multiple reconstruction surgeries. I immediately look back at the photo.

doubletake

Seeing no evidence, it made me wonder whether I'd be so eager to check her appearance had the woman survived a brain tumor.

one breast

This is how I participate in my own gender surveillance. Does it show?

after another

the anorexic's
last resort
chemical peel

bonsai
the hips on a jack pine
shaped into service

dame's rocket
the purple bruising
left in her wake

It's after 7pm and the heat's finally dissipated enough to consider taking a jog around the Basilica of San Giovanni. In August the air quality isn't too bad since most Romans drive their diesel out of the city for a few weeks of polluting elsewhere. So I lace up my sneakers and head out.

Stations of the Cross

Pausing at a light, a white electric Fiat pulls up next to me. The driver gets out and waves, saying something about a man he saw following me for the last few blocks. The walk sign is on but I'm still on the curb trying to understand the driver's thick regional dialect.

after each stop

I ask where the man is now and he points down the street behind us. The driver steps onto the sidewalk. He says I need to be careful. He offers to give me a ride home.

a candle blown out

plantation
the   path   away
        from

               the

                    shacks

where the no**o**se hung

the shadow side of the oak

exposed bedrock
the all-white jury

acquits

from sheets to Klan robes the whites of their eyes

plantation stubble field the white bones

a
few swallows
a
knee
a
neck

frustration of a black man

who can't get blue in the face

shifting tones
of urban renewal
a winning bid
to paint the condos
blackened white

c
h
i
m
n
e
y
s

long shadows
over Dachau

at war
with his blanket
my father relives
his nights
in the trenches

raising the rifle
to sight the deer
the cross
around his neck
shifts to the right

wolf moon
papering the windows
for the Ave Maria

their encampment
behind
the church
the indulgence
of a La-Z-Boy

flattened boxes another night squeezed out in the alley

air raid shelter
the quieter callings
of stray cats and doves

ten o'clock curfew
ending the protest
hunger moon

line at the food bank
        the distance
   between meals

vanishing white
a polar bear dissolves
in the distance

clear cut
a woodpecker forages
sideways

higher tides
crabs scuttling
on asphalt

uprising
a thousand monarchs
take over a tree

zigzag hummingbirds
the circular rhythm
of razor wire

new nesting material the Target logo

ACKNOWLEDGMENTS

I owe a debt of gratitude to Jim Kacian for bringing this work to fruition; his wise counsel and design expertise in creating this collection were invaluable. Many thanks also to Kristen Lindquist and Alan Summers, for their careful reading and generous encouragement as the project took shape. Finally, I owe the world to both my husband Carl Liebold, who lovingly offers the perfect alignment of his left brain to my right; and to my sister Pene, for her deep compassion and stunning clarity of aesthetic vision.

Kind thanks to the editors and publishers of the following publications in which present or earlier versions of many of these pieces first appeared:

#FemkuMag, Autumn Moon, bones, bottle rockets press, brass bell, Cold Moon, Failed Haiku, Frogpond, Kingfisher, Mariposa, Modern Haiku, Nick Virgilio Haiku in Action, *North Carolina Poetry Society Pinesong Awards Anthology, Poetry Pea, Presence,* The Haiku Foundation Haiku Dialogue, *The Haiku Way to Healing Anthology, (ed.* Robert Epstein), *The Heron's Nest,* tinywords, *Trash Panda, tsuri-dōrō,* and *weird laburnum.* "Vanishing Point," originally published in *Frogpond*, also appeared in *Contemporary Haibun* 17. "exposed bedrock" was awarded an Honorable Mention in the North Carolina Poetry Society 2022 Bloodroot Haiku contest. "vanishing white" received an Honorable Mention in the First International Modern Kigo Competition held in February, 2022.

AUTHOR'S NOTE

This collection emerged from my ongoing relationship with Zen Peacemakers International, a global organization whose members and affiliates mobilize peace-building, humanitarian, social, and civic action. Check out www.zenpeacemakers.org to learn more.

I offer these poems as an act of bearing witness.

May they inspire compassionate action.